Simply Stylish

Chain & Metal Jewelry

From the publisher of *BeadStyle* magazine

KALMBACH BOOKS

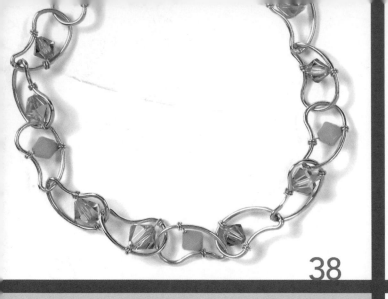

38

55

Kalmbach Books
21027 Crossroads Circle
Waukesha, Wisconsin 53186
www.Kalmbach.com/Books

Published in 2010
14 13 12 11 10   1 2 3 4 5

Manufactured in the United States of America

ISBN: 978-0-87116-297-7

The material in this book has appeared previously in *BeadStyle* magazine. *BeadStyle* is registered as a trademark.

Publisher's Cataloging-in-Publication Data

Simply stylish chain & metal jewelry / from the publisher of BeadStyle magazine.

    p. : col. ill. ; cm.

    ISBN: 978-0-87116-297-7

1. Chains (Jewelry)--Design--Handbooks, manuals, etc.
2. Copper jewelry)--Design--Handbooks, manuals, etc.
3. Silver jewelry)--Design--Handbooks, manuals, etc.
4. Jewelry making--Handbooks, manuals, etc. I. Title: Simply stylish chain and metal jewelry II. Title: Chain & metal jewelry III. Title: BeadStyle magazine.

TT212 .S566 2010
739.27

TABLE OF CONTENTS

67

78

Introduction

There's no denying the ongoing popularity of metal and chain as beading and jewelry-making materials. The clean lines and elegant drape of chain jewelry are beautifully versatile, and the urban gleam of metal beads, spacers, charms, and pendants can be used to accent everything from jeans to an evening gown.

That's why this collection is so great: It brings you the best editor-tested designs using chain and metal that *BeadStyle* has to offer. In the 30 projects that fill the following pages, you'll learn how to string pearls with chain in an uncommon combination (p. 36), how to make your own bohemian chain-and-chandelier earrings (p. 43), and even how to patinate your metals and chain for an antiqued look (p. 18 and p. 58). All the hottest styles are represented. Layered chains, mixed metals — it's all here, along with clear directions, a guide to chain styles, and a basic techniques and tools section.

But these jewelry designs aren't just wearable, they're doable, too. All the projects are beginner-level and require no special metalworking tools or skills. And you don't need to be a chain mail artist, either — most of the chain used in the book can be bought preassembled.

Cool and classy or fun and funky, yards of chain and heaps of metal beads come together here for a simple and stylish collection of jewelry projects.

Basics

Cutting flexible beading wire

Decide how long you want your necklace to be. Add 6 in. (15cm) and cut a piece of beading wire to that length. (For a bracelet, add 5 in./13cm.)

Plain loop

1 Trim the wire ⅜ in. (1cm) above the top bead. Make a right-angle bend close to the bead.
2 Grab the wire's tip with roundnose pliers. Roll the wire to form a half circle. Release the wire.
3 Reposition the pliers in the loop and continue rolling, forming a centered circle above the bead.
4 The finished loop.

Opening a jump ring or loop

1 Hold the jump ring or loop with chainnose and roundnose pliers or two pairs of chainnose pliers.
2 To open the jump ring or loop, bring one pair of pliers toward you. Reverse the steps to close.

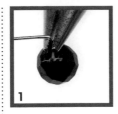 

Wrapped loop

1 Make sure there is at least 1¼ in. (3.2cm) of wire above the bead. With the tip of your chainnose pliers, grasp the wire directly above the bead. Bend the wire (above the pliers) into a right angle.
2 Position the jaws of your roundnose pliers vertically in the bend.
3 Bring the wire over the top jaw of the pliers.
4 Reposition the pliers' lower jaw snugly in the curved wire. Wrap the wire down and around the bottom of the pliers. This is the first half of a wrapped loop.
5 Grasp the loop with chainnose pliers.
6 Wrap the wire tail around the wire stem, covering the stem between the loop and the top bead. Trim the excess wrapping wire, and press the end close to the stem with chainnose or crimping pliers.

Flattened crimp

1 Hold the crimp bead with the tip of your chainnose pliers. Squeeze the pliers firmly to flatten the crimp bead. Tug the clasp to make sure the crimp has a solid grip on the wire. If the wire slides, remove the crimp bead and repeat the steps with a new crimp bead.
2 Tug on the wire to be sure the flattened crimp is secure.

Folded crimp

1 Position the crimp bead in the notch closest to the crimping pliers' handle.
2 Separate the wires and firmly squeeze the crimp bead.
3 Move the crimp bead into the notch at the pliers' tip. Squeeze the pliers, folding the bead in half at the indentation.
4 Tug on the wire to be sure the folded crimp is secure.

Basics

Tools

End crimp
1 Glue one end of the cord and place it in a crimp end. Use chainnose pliers to fold one side of the crimp end over the cord.
2 Repeat with the second side of the crimp end and squeeze gently.

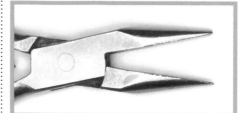

Chainnose pliers have smooth, flat inner jaws, and the tips taper to a point. Use them for gripping and for opening and closing loops and jump rings.

Use **split-ring pliers** to simplify opening split rings by inserting a curved jaw between the wires.

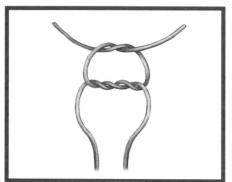

Surgeon's knot
Cross the right end over the left and go through the loop. Go through again. Cross the left end over the right and go through. Pull the ends to tighten the knot.

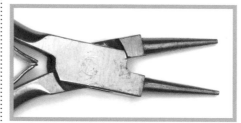

Roundnose pliers have smooth, tapered, conical jaws used to make loops. The closer to the tip you work, the smaller the loop will be.

A **hammer** is used to harden wire for hoops and bangles. Any hammer with a flat head will work, as long as the head is free of nicks that could mar your metal. The light ball-peen hammer shown here is one of the most commonly used hammers for jewelry making.

Crimping pliers have two grooves in their jaws that are used to fold or roll a crimp bead into a compact shape.

Overhand knot
Make a loop and pass the working end through it. Pull the ends to tighten the knot.

With **diagonal wire cutters,** use the front of the blades to make a pointed cut and the back of the blades to make a flat cut.

A **bench block** provides a hard, smooth surface on which to hammer your pieces. An anvil is similarly hard but has different surfaces, such as a tapered horn, to help form wire into different shapes.

Materials

Clasps come in many sizes and shapes. Some of the most common are the lobster claw, which opens when you pull a tiny lever; toggle, consisting of a ring and a bar; hook-and-eye, consisting of a hook and a jump ring or split ring; slide, consisting of one tube that slides inside another; and S-hook, which links two soldered jump rings or split rings.

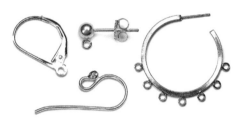

Earring findings come in a variety of metals and styles, including post, French hook, lever-back, and hoop. You will almost always want a loop (or loops) on earring findings so you can attach beads.

Crimp beads are small, large-holed, thin-walled metal beads designed to be flattened or crimped into a tight roll. Use them when stringing jewelry on flexible beading wire. **Crimp bead covers** provide a way to hide your crimps by covering them with a finding that mimics the look of a small bead.

Spacers are small beads used between larger beads to space the placement of the beads.

A **jump ring** is used to connect two components. It is a small wire circle or oval that is either soldered or comes with an opening. **Split rings** are used like jump rings but are much more secure. They look like tiny key rings and are made of springy wire.

A **head pin** looks like a long, thick, blunt sewing pin. It has a flat or decorative head on one end to keep beads on. Head pins come in different diameters (or gauges) and lengths. **Eye pins** are just like head pins except they have a round loop on one end instead of a head. You can make your own eye pins from wire.

Flexible beading wire is composed of steel wires twisted together and covered with nylon. This wire is much stronger than thread and does not stretch; the higher the number of inner strands (between three and 49), the more flexible and kink-resistant the wire. It is available in a variety of sizes.

Crimp ends and **pinch ends** are used to connect the ends of leather, ribbons, or other fiber lacing materials to a clasp.

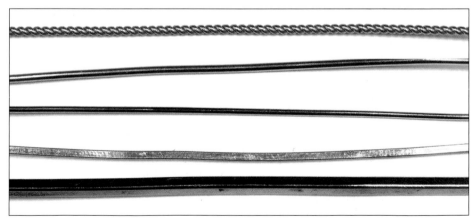

Wire is available in a number of materials and finishes, including brass, gold, gold-filled, gold-plated, fine silver, sterling silver, anodized niobium (chemically colored wire), and copper. Brass, copper, and craft wire are packaged in 10–40-yd. (9.5–36.6m) spools, while gold, silver, and niobium are usually sold by the foot or ounce. Wire thickness is measured by gauge — the higher the gauge, the thinner the wire — and is available in varying hardnesses and shapes, including twisted, round, half-round, and square.

Metal & Chain

Metal types

Findings (like bead caps and cones, clasps, earring wires, and spacers) as well as wire and chain choices, may be available in several types of metal.

Metals may be precious, like gold, silver, platinum, and rhodium, or base, like brass, copper, gunmetal, pewter, niobium, and titanium. If you like the look of precious metals but not the price, you might try pieces that have been plated, filled, finished, or washed with gold or silver. "Plated" means a very thin layer of gold or silver has been electroplated or electrochemically applied to another metal. "Filled" refers to a layer of gold or silver applied to a cheaper material (usually brass) with heat and pressure. And "finished" (or "washed") means a base metal has been electroplated with a non-standardized thickness of gold or silver.

Adding a patina

If you like an antiqued look, there are several different techniques you can try on your metal and chain jewelry. Steven James's project, "Antique technique" (p. 18), demonstrates using a packaged blackening product to antique your jewelry, while Jane Konkel's "Create a cool patina" (p. 58) uses ammonia for a blue finish on copper. Other pieces, like Gretta Van Someren's mixed metal earrings (p. 46), can be oxidized with liver of sulfur, or by sealing your jewelry in an airtight container with a cooked egg yolk.

Chain types

Chain is available in many finishes, including sterling silver and gold-filled as well as base metal or plated metals. Different styles include:

curb

figaro

long and short

rolo

cable

Simply Stylish
Necklaces

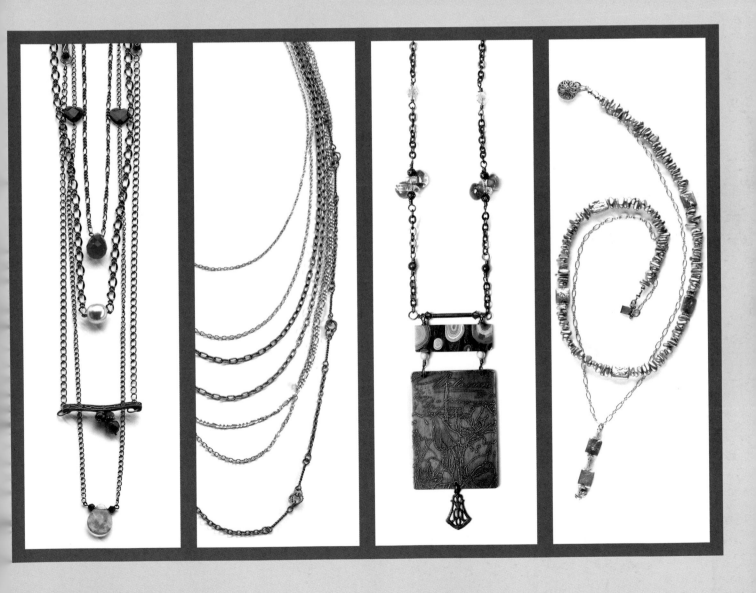

Chain reigns

Combine a variety of chains in an extra-long necklace

by Rupa Balachandar

This flapper-style necklace boasts four chains in different sizes, styles, and finishes. Keep the number of beads, charms, and vintage components to a minimum, and then stagger them so the long, lean links remain the focus.

SupplyList

necklace: longest strand
36 in. (91cm), shortest
strand 30 in. (76cm)

- 10–12 ft. (3–3.7m) chain
  in four styles and finishes,
  28–38 in. (71–97cm) of
  each
- **8–12** 12–40mm assorted
  charms with hanging
  loops, beads, and vintage
  components
- 10–15 in. (25–38cm)
  22-gauge half-hard wire
  (2½ in./6.4cm per bead)
- **10–25** 4mm jump rings
- **2** 5mm jump rings
- toggle clasp or S-hook
  clasp
- chainnose piers
- roundnose pliers
- diagonal wire cutters

1 a Determine the finished length of the shortest chain of your necklace and cut a piece to that length. Cut three more pieces of chain, each 2 in. (5cm) longer than the previous one. (These chains are 30, 32, 34, and 36 in./ 76, 81, 86, and 91cm respectively.)

b Arrange the beads and vintage components along the chains, balancing colors, finishes, shapes, and sizes.

c To make a bead unit, cut a 2½-in. (6.4cm) piece of wire. Make a plain loop (Basics, p. 5) at one end. String a bead on the wire and make a plain loop at the other end.

2 a For the chain with one bead unit, cut the chain into two equal-length pieces. Open a loop on the bead unit and attach the loop to the chain. Close the loop. Repeat on the other side of the bead unit.

b For the chain with three bead units, cut the chain into four equal-length pieces. Attach bead units as in step 2a.

3 a For the chain with three vintage components, cut the chain into four pieces. Open two jump rings and attach each end of one component to a chain. Close the jump rings. Repeat with the remaining components and pieces of chain.

b For the chain with the charm, cut the chain into two equal-length pieces. Open a jump ring (Basics) and attach the charm's loop and each chain. Close the jump ring.

4 If necessary, trim each chain within 1 in. (2.5cm) of the desired length. Open a 5mm jump ring. Attach one end of each chain to the jump ring and half of a clasp. Close the jump ring. Repeat on the other end.

An etched
copper pendant
falls from a
moonlit sky

by Lorelei Eurto

The holes of Jennifer Stumpf's etched copper pendant line up perfectly with the holes of Heather Powers' Starry Night cuff bead. A few colorful drops, rounds, and rondelles mimic the night sky filled with swirling clouds, blazing stars, and the bright moon of Van Gogh's masterpiece.

Starry night

1 Cut two 3-in. (7.6cm) pieces of wire. On one end of each wire, make the first half of a wrapped loop (Basics, p. 5). Attach a corner hole of the pendant and complete the wraps.

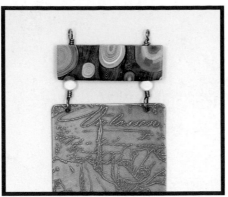

2 On each wire, string a 4mm bead and an outer hole of a cuff bead. Make a wrapped loop.

3 Cut a 4-in. (10cm) piece of wire and make a wrapped loop. String: loop of the cuff bead, 4mm, tube bead, 4mm, remaining loop of the cuff bead. Make a wrapped loop.

4 Cut a 3-in. (7.6cm) piece of wire and make a wrapped loop. String one to four beads and make a wrapped loop. Make eight to 10 bead units.

5 Cut ten or twelve ½–2½-in. (1.3–6.4cm) pieces of chain. Open the link (Basics) of a short piece of chain and attach a loop of the tube unit. Close the link. Repeat on the other side.

SupplyList

necklace 21 in. (53cm)
- 42mm etched copper pendant with three holes (Jennifer Stumpf, jenniferstumpf.etsy.com)
- 36mm Starry Night cuff bead (Heather Powers, humblebeads.com)
- 18–30mm tube bead
- 12–18mm charm and jump ring
- **4** 10mm boro glass beads (Unicorne Beads, unicornebeads.com)
- **14–18** 4–8mm beads
- 34–40 in. (86–100cm) 22-gauge Artistic Wire
- 14–18 in. (36–46cm) chain, 3mm links
- 14mm hook-and-eye clasp
- chainnose pliers
- roundnose pliers
- diagonal wire cutters

6 On each side, open the end link of the chain and attach a bead unit. Close the link. Continue attaching chains and bead units until your necklace is within ½ in. (1.3cm) of the finished length.

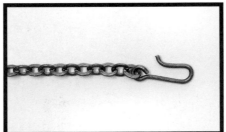

7 Check the fit, and trim chain from each end if necessary. On each end, attach half of a clasp. Open a jump ring (Basics) and attach a charm and the center hole of the pendant. Close the jump ring.

TIP
Choose a tube bead that is the approximate length of your cuff bead (30mm). If you choose a shorter tube, string beads on each end of the tube in step 3 to make up the difference.

DESIGN ALTERNATIVE
This necklace pairs a brass etched pendant with cuff and disk beads inspired by Claude Monet, and uses fancy copper and brass chain instead of attaching bead units to links of chain.

The bead-and-chain
diet

Create a slimming jewelry piece

by Erin Dolan

While short, chunky styles add bulk, a long necklace creates a lean line that gives the illusion of height. This extra-long lariat goes a long way toward elongating a shorter torso.

1 On a head pin, string a crystal. Make a plain loop (Basics, p. 5). Make 90 to 110 crystal units.

2 Decide how long you want your lariat to be and cut a piece of chain to that length. Open the loop of a crystal unit (Basics) and attach it to the center link of the chain. Close the loop. Attach six to eight more crystal units to the center link.

3 On each side of the center link, skip five links and attach three crystal units to the next link. Continue attaching crystal units, leaving five links open between each cluster. Leave the last 10 to 15 links open on each end.

4 On each end, attach six to 10 crystal units to the last three chain links.

Supply List

lariat 60 in. (1.5m)
- **90–110** 3–8mm assorted crystals
- **4–5** ft. (1.2–1.5m) chain, 10–12mm links
- **90–110** 2-in. (5cm) 22-gauge head pins
- chainnose pliers
- roundnose pliers
- diagonal wire cutters

DESIGN ALTERNATIVE
String crystals and seed beads on beading wire for a shorter, less time-consuming lariat. For a 32-in. (81cm) lariat, you'll need 100 to 125 crystals.

TIPS
- Make your plain loops large enough so they can easily fit around the chain links.
- If your loops are too small or if you want a more uniform lariat, attach the crystal units in each cluster to a jump ring. Then, attach the jump ring to the chain link.
- The lariat's length makes it a versatile piece. Fold it in half and slide both ends through the fold, or loop the ends in a loose knot.

Trinkets
from the deep

This necklace captures the romance of sunken treasure

by Brenda Schweder

This eclectic mix of chains and trinkets could be from a treasure hunter's stash. Tie on a multitone shell and a stamped tag for a stylish necklace that suggests a murky nautical backstory.

1 Cut an 18-in. (46cm) piece of round-link chain and two 18-in. (46cm) pieces of plastic chain. Cut two 12-in. (30cm) pieces of cord. On one end of the three chains, center the end links on a cord and tie two overhand knots (Basics, p. 5). Repeat on the other end.

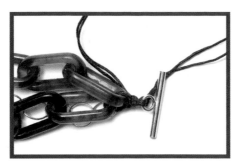

2 On each end, tie half of a clasp to the cord with two overhand knots. Tie an overhand knot on each end of each cord 2½ in. (6.4cm) from the clasp. Trim the excess cord.

Supply List

necklace 18½ in. (47cm)
- 2-in. (5cm) notched shell pendant
- 1-in. (2.5cm) metal tag
- 4 ft. (1.2m) waxed linen cord
- 18 in. (46cm) round-link chain, 10mm links
- 37 in. (94cm) plastic chain, ¾-in. (1.9cm) links (Laramie Studios, vintagebeadslaramiestudios.com)
- toggle clasp
- diagonal wire cutters

3 Cut a 24-in. (61cm) piece of cord and fold it in half. Wrap the folded cord around the shell so the loop is positioned over the notch. String the ends through the loop.

4 Wrap the cord around the shell and through the loop a second time. Tighten the cord and tie two overhand knots next to the shell.

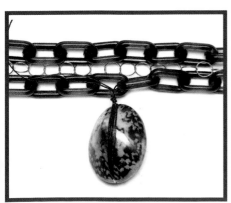

5 Tie two overhand knots to attach the shell to the sixth link of one of the plastic chains.

6 Tie two surgeon's knots (Basics) to attach the tag to the shell dangle. Trim the ends about 1 in. (2.5cm) from the knots.

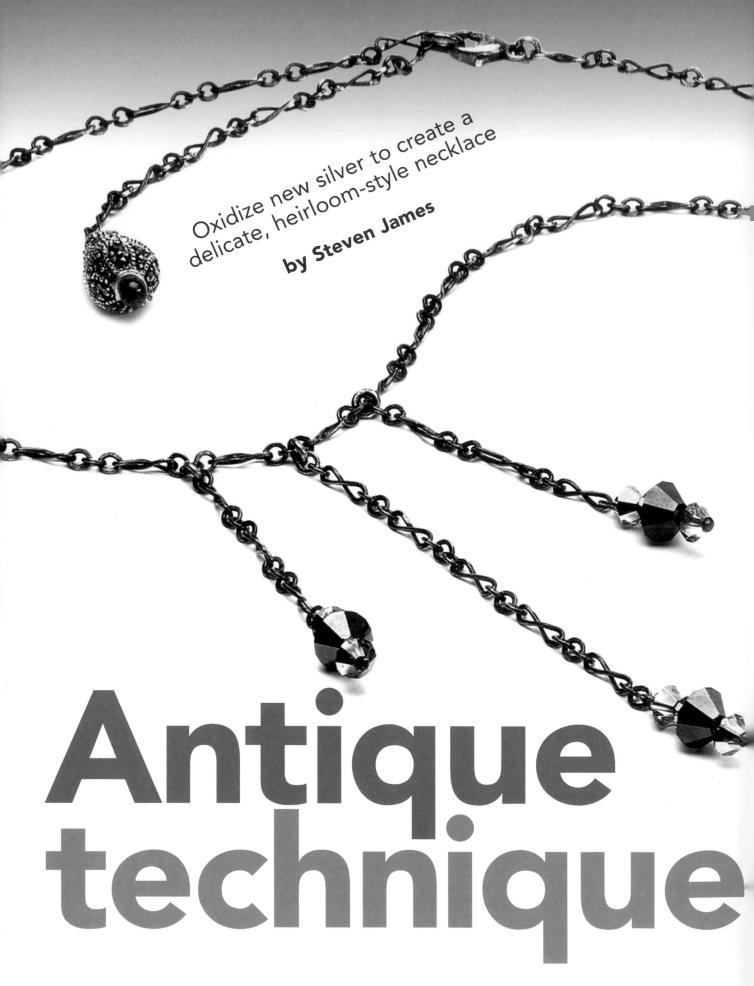

Oxidize new silver to create a delicate, heirloom-style necklace

by Steven James

Antique technique

Transform a shiny, contemporary necklace into one with the mysterious air of a bygone era. The secret lies in a 15-second process that alters new silver, producing a dramatic metamorphosis.

1 Determine the finished length of your necklace. Cut a piece of chain to the necklace length, cutting through a long link of chain. Cut two 2½-in. (6cm) and two 1¼-in. (3cm) lengths of chain for the dangles. Gather all the sterling silver components.

2 Read the Black Max directions thoroughly. Following the directions, dip the chain, jump rings, spacers, clasp, and head pins in the solution for 15 seconds. Remove the items and wash with a mild detergent. Rinse the pieces and let them dry completely. Use a furniture polish wipe to apply a light coat of wax; this protects the black finish.

SupplyList

necklace 15 in. (38cm) with a 3-in. (7.6cm) dangle
- 2 ft. (61cm) sterling silver chain, 3mm triple long and short
- 3 6mm bicone crystals
- 6 4mm bicone crystals
- 6 x 14mm teardrop-shaped bead, marcasite
- 4mm spacer bead, sterling silver
- 3mm spacer bead, sterling silver
- 4 1½-in. (38mm) head pins, sterling silver
- 4 3mm jump rings, sterling silver
- lobster claw clasp and 5mm jump ring, sterling silver
- chainnose pliers
- roundnose pliers
- diagonal wire cutters
- Midas Black Max (Rio Grande, riogrande.com)
- pre-moistened furniture polish wipe, such as Pledge Wipes

3 String a head pin with a 4mm crystal, a 6mm crystal, and a 4mm crystal. Make a plain loop (Basics, p. 5). Repeat for a total of three dangles. Open the loops and attach one dangle to each 1¼-in. chain segment and one to a 2½-in. chain segment. Close the loops.

4 Open a 3mm jump ring (Basics) and attach the 2½-in. dangle to the center of the necklace. Close the jump ring. Use a 3mm jump ring to attach each of the two 1¼-in. dangles to the middle link of the small-link section of chain on each side of the center dangle.

5 String a head pin with a 3mm spacer, a marcasite drop, and a 4mm spacer. Make the first half of a wrapped loop (Basics) above the top bead. Slide the dangle onto the end link of the remaining 2½-in. piece of chain. Complete the wraps and trim the excess wire. Dab a bit of Black Max on the cut end of the wire. Be careful not to get Black Max on the marcasite.

6 Open a 3mm jump ring and attach a lobster claw clasp to one end of the necklace chain. Close the jump ring.

7 Open the 5mm jump ring and attach it to the other end of the necklace and the end link of the marcasite drop. Close the jump ring.

Patina process

- Use sterling silver components; the effect isn't the same with base metal or plated pieces.

- Use Black Max, Silver Black, liver of sulfur, or chlorine to chemically oxidize the silver. Each chemical produces a slightly different result. Use a polishing pad or fine-gauge steel wool to remove some of the black for a two-tone effect.

- To oxidize naturally, seal the silver and half a hard-boiled egg in a plastic bag and refrigerate overnight. Make sure the silver doesn't touch the egg.

Double take

Create a clever two-tiered necklace

Chain pairs with a beaded strand in an interesting dichotomy: Luminous coin pearls hang from delicate chain, then reappear within the shorter beaded strand. This layered design invites a second look.

by Rupa Balachandar

SupplyList

chain strand 18 in. (46cm), beaded strand 17 in. (43cm)

- 16-in. (41cm) strand 6–8mm gemstone chips or keshi pearls
- **7** 12mm coin pearls, round or rectangular
- **18** 5mm flat spacers
- **2** 1½-in. (3.8cm) eye pins
- **2** 1½-in. head pins
- **5** 4 x 5mm oval jump rings
- **4** 3mm round spacer beads
- **2** crimp beads
- two-strand box clasp with attached jump rings
- 20 in. (51cm) 1.6mm long-and-short chain
- flexible beading wire, .014 or .015
- chainnose pliers
- roundnose pliers
- diagonal wire cutters
- crimping pliers (optional)

1 Determine the finished length of your necklace. Cut a piece of beading wire (Basics, p. 5). Cut a piece of chain to the desired length. String a chip on a head pin. Make a plain loop (Basics) above the chip. Make a second dangle.

2 String a flat spacer, a coin pearl, and a flat spacer on an eye pin. Make a wrapped loop (Basics) above the top spacer, perpendicular to the bottom loop. Make a second pearl component.

3 Open the loop on a pearl component and string the two chip dangles. Close the loop. Open the loop of the second pearl component and string the wrapped loop of the first pearl component. Close the loop. Open a jump ring (Basics) and attach the entire dangle. Close the jump ring and center the dangle on the chain.

4 String a flat spacer, a pearl, and a flat spacer on the beading wire.

5 On each end of the wire, string 10 chips, a spacer, and 10 chips.

6 Repeat steps 4 and 5 once more, then step 4 again, on each end. String chips until the necklace is within 1 in. (2.5cm) of the desired length.

7 Open four jump rings. Attach one to each one of a clasp's jump rings. Close the jump rings. On each end of the beaded strand, string a round spacer, a crimp bead, a round spacer, and a jump ring just attached to the clasp. Go back through the beads just strung plus one or two more and tighten the wire. Check the fit, and add or remove beads from each end if necessary. Crimp the crimp beads (Basics) and trim the excess wire. Open the remaining jump rings and attach each end link of chain. Close the jump rings. If necessary, trim the chain.

TIP
To make eye pins, trim the head from a head pin and make a plain loop at one end, or make a plain loop on the end of a 2-in. (5cm) piece of 22-gauge wire.

SHOW YOUR METAL

Create mixed-metal necklaces with chains, washers, and double-circle components

by Naomi Fujimoto

Whether you take the straight-and-narrow path or venture the roundabout way, be fearless in mixing your metals. The multistrand necklace features delicate chains in silver, gold, brass, copper, and gunmetal. For a gentle drape, use extra-fine chain in a variety of styles, such as cable, figaro, or bar-and-link. Or, if you prefer circular reasoning, connect washers and double-circle components for a modern, geometric choker. You'll love the simplicity and clean lines of both necklaces.

TIP
Store the chain necklace on a hanger to prevent tangling. If your necklace gets tangled, open the jump ring on one side, remove the chains, and untangle them. Replace the chains and close the jump ring.

1 **metal-component necklace • **Open a 4 x 5mm oval jump ring (Basics, p. 5). Attach the 22mm washer and a hole in a solid double-circle component. Close the jump ring. Repeat on the other side, attaching an open-center double-circle component.

2 On each end, use a jump ring to attach a 10mm washer to the remaining hole in the double-circle component.

Use a jump ring to attach a solid or open-center double-circle component to each washer.

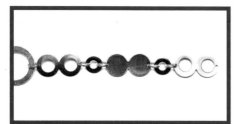

3 Repeat step 2, alternating solid and open-center components on each side, until the necklace is within 1 in. (2.5cm) of the desired length.

4 Use a jump ring to attach half of a clasp to each end. Check the fit, and add or remove an equal number of washers or components from each end if necessary. To lengthen the necklace only slightly, attach an extra jump ring to each end.

1 **multichain necklace • **Determine the finished length of your necklace. Cut a piece of chain to the shortest length. Cut subsequent chains each 1 in. (2.5cm) longer than the previous piece. To emphasize the top and bottom chains, cut the second and last chains approximately 2 in. (5cm) longer than the previous piece.

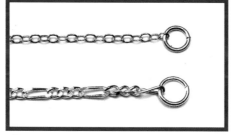

2 For chains with 1.5–2mm links, open a 3mm jump ring (Basics) and attach it to one end of the chain. Repeat on the other end.

3 Use 4 x 5mm oval jump rings to attach one end of each chain to half of a clasp. Check the fit, and trim the chains if necessary. To lengthen the necklace, attach extra jump rings to each end.

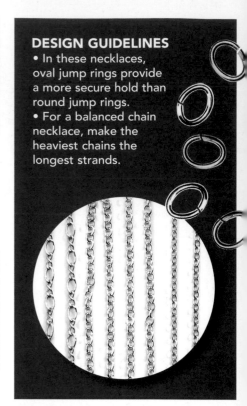

Supply List

metal-component necklace 16 in. (41cm)
• 22mm silver washer (Metalliferous, metalliferous.com)
• **10–12** 25mm brass double-circle two-hole components, **5–6** each of solid and open-center (Metalliferous)
• **8–10** 10mm silver washers
• **20–26** 4 x 5mm oval jump rings
• toggle clasp
• chainnose and roundnose pliers, or two pairs of chainnose pliers

multichain necklace: shortest strand 14¼ in. (36.2cm), longest strand 22½ in. (57.2cm)
• 15–26 in. (38–66cm) each of **6 or 7** kinds of chain, 1.5–4mm links
• **2–6** 4 x 5mm oval jump rings
• **2–14** 3mm jump rings (in metals to match the 1.5–2mm-link chains)
• toggle clasp
• chainnose and roundnose pliers, or **2** pairs of chainnose pliers
• diagonal or heavy-duty wire cutters

Simply Stylish
Bracelets

Beau jangles

Wire dainty beads to metal bangle bracelets for up-to-the-minute style

by Brenda Schweder

Although these baubles are timeless, bracelets are particularly au courant when embellished with tiny beads. Try a single silver sliver, or wire two or three together and stack an armful. Both fun and refined, these wire trinkets add a great twist to your style.

Supply List

bracelets
- assorted 2–4mm gemstones and crystals
- **3** or more 60–63mm bangle bracelets
- 22-gauge wire, half hard
- spool of 30-gauge wire
- chainnose pliers
- diagonal wire cutters

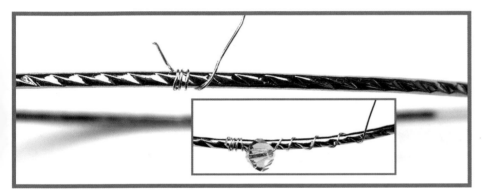

1 Cut a 30-in. (76cm) piece of 30-gauge wire. Wrap one end around a bangle tightly three or four times. Trim the excess wire. String a bead and wrap the wire around the bangle every ⅛ in. (3mm) or so. String beads at ½-in. (1.3cm) intervals or as desired. To finish, make several wraps around the bangle. Trim the excess wire.

2 Cut a 1½-in. (3.8cm) piece of 22-gauge wire. Stack the beaded bangle with one or two plain bangles. Positioning the wire between two beads, tightly wrap around all the bangles two or three times. Trim the excess wire from both ends and gently squeeze each end down with chainnose pliers. Repeat one or two times around the bangle.

Mix assorted chains with a round focal piece for a prize bracelet

Grab the

brass ring

by Brenda Schweder

An etched free-form circle, or even a vintage belt ring, makes a great focal piece for a mixed-chain bracelet. The best part is, you don't have to worry about matching all your findings. Dare to pair a silver jump ring with a brass clasp, or incorporate old metals with new for a winning combination.

1 Open a 7–10mm jump ring (Basics, p. 5). String an end link of each of the six chains. Wrap the chains around the focal component and string a link of each chain on the jump ring. Close the jump ring and trim the excess chain.

2 Use a 5mm jump ring to attach metal charms to the 7–10mm jump ring.

3 Determine the finished length of your bracelet, subtract the diameter of the focal component, and divide that number in half. Cut two pieces of each chain to that length. Use a 5mm jump ring to attach one set of chains to the 7–10mm jump ring. Set aside the other set of chains.

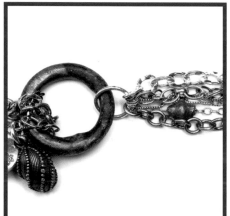

4 Open a 10–12mm jump ring. Attach the remaining set of chains and the focal component. If the component has an attached loop, use a 5mm jump ring to attach the chains to the loop. String a large-hole metal accent bead on the finest chain.

5 Use a 5mm jump ring to attach the working end of each set of chains to half of a clasp. Check the fit, and trim the chains or attach an additional jump ring if necessary.

TIP
When wrapping chain around the focal component, close the jump ring before trimming the excess chain. This is easier than trying to connect short pieces of chain with a jump ring.

Win a silver metal

Make a sterling silver bracelet in under 30 minutes

by Nina Cooper

String a contemporary bracelet that pairs puffy metal disks with tiny, pale crystals. Alternate printed and matte beads; you'll love the juxtaposition of graphic patterns and smooth silver.

1 bracelet • Cut a piece of beading wire (Basics, p. 5). String a printed bead, a crystal, a matte bead, and a crystal. Repeat until the bracelet is within 1 in. (2.5cm) of the desired length. End with a printed or matte bead.

2 On each end, string a spacer, a crimp bead, a spacer, and half of the clasp. Go back through the beads just strung and tighten the wire. Check the fit, and add or remove beads if necessary. Crimp the crimp beads (Basics) and trim the excess wire.

SupplyList

bracelet 7–9½ in. (18–24.1cm)
- **10–13** 13mm silver disk beads, in matte and printed styles
- **10–13** 3mm bicone crystals
- **4** 3mm silver spacers
- flexible beading wire, .014 or .015
- **2** crimp beads
- toggle clasp
- chainnose or crimping pliers
- diagonal wire cutters

HARDWARE

by Lindsay Haedt

Link common washers into an uncommonly fashionable bracelet

This chunky collection of rings and washers comes together in a substantial bracelet with a value beyond the sum of its parts. Washers are easy to find and easy to afford — it's the designer's eye that makes the end results anything but common.

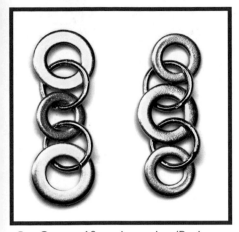

1 a Open a 10mm jump ring (Basics, p. 5). Attach a 6mm washer and a 5mm washer. Close the jump ring. Use a jump ring to attach the 5mm washer to another 6mm washer. Make a total of four units.

b Attach a 5mm washer to a 6mm washer. Attach the 6mm washer to another 5mm washer. Make a total of three units.

2 Arrange washer units in a row, alternating the two types. Begin and end with units that have a 5mm washer in the middle. Use jump rings to attach the washers in one unit to the respective washers in the next unit until all units are connected. Check the fit, allowing 3½ in. (8.9cm) for finishing. Add or remove units if necessary.

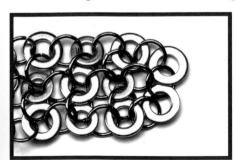

3 Use a jump ring to connect two 6mm washers. Repeat. Using three jump rings, attach each 6mm unit (including the jump ring) to the respective washers on each side.

4 Use a jump ring to attach two 5mm washers. Repeat. Attach each unit (excluding the jump ring) to the respective washers on each side. Attach a 5mm washer to each remaining jump ring.

On each end, attach a split ring to the 5mm washer (Basics). On one end, attach a lobster claw clasp to the split ring.

SUPPLY NOTE
At home-improvement stores, washers are measured by their inside diameters. The 5mm and 6mm washers have 10mm and 12mm outside diameters, respectively.

Supply List

bracelet 7–8 in. (18–20cm)
- **11–17** 6mm washers
- **13–19** 5mm washers
- **36–56** 10mm jump rings
- **2** 6–8mm split rings
- lobster claw clasp
- chainnose and roundnose pliers, or **2** pairs chainnose pliers
- split-ring pliers (optional)

Chained pearls

Pearls and a variety of links draw attention

by Julie Boonshaft

Classic pearls lend this bracelet a sophisticated look, while chains in several shades of silver give it mesmerizing depth. Mix bright chains with patinated silver or gunmetal so each strand has a unique identity, but use chain with links of similar shape to create unity.

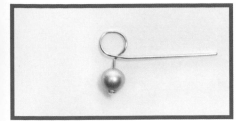 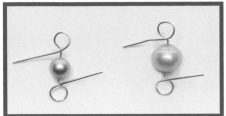

1 On a head pin, string a 4–5mm pearl. Make the first half of a wrapped loop (Basics, p. 5). Make seven pearl dangles.

2 Cut a 2-in. (5cm) piece of wire and make the first half of a wrapped loop on one end. String a 4–5mm pearl and make the first half of a wrapped loop. Make 11 4–5mm pearl connectors and five 6–7mm pearl connectors.

SupplyList

bracelet 8 in. (20cm)
- **5** 6–7mm pearls
- **18** 4–5mm pearls
- 32 in. (81cm) 24-gauge wire
- 7 in. (18cm) chain, 11–13mm links
- 5½ in. (14cm) chain, 8–10mm links
- 4 in. (10cm) chain, 4–7mm links
- 5 in. (13cm) chain, 2–3mm links
- **7** 2-in. (5cm) head pins
- 16–18mm lobster claw clasp
- chainnose pliers
- roundnose pliers
- diagonal wire cutters

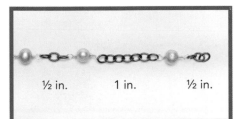 

3 Cut a 7-in. (18cm) piece of 11–13mm link chain and a 5½-in. (14cm) piece of 8–10mm link chain. Attach six pearl dangles to the 8–10mm chain. Complete the wraps as you go.

DESIGN ALTERNATIVE
Too much chain for your taste? Reverse the chain-to-pearl ratio with a two-strand bracelet, a few links of chain, and pearls in similar colors. Multicolor pearl strand from Rings & Things, rings-things.com.

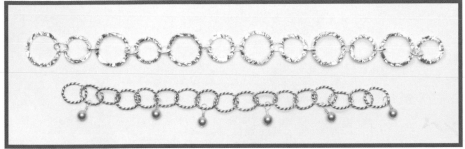
½ in.   1 in.   ½ in.

4 Cut three ½-in. (1.3cm) and two 1-in. (2.5cm) pieces of 4–7mm link chain. Attach a 6–7mm pearl connector to each end of a ½-in. (1.3cm) chain. On each end, attach a 1-in. (2.5cm) chain, a 6–7mm pearl connector, and a ½-in. (1.3cm) chain. Complete the wraps as you go.

5 Cut six ½–¾-in. (1.3–1.9cm) pieces of 2–3mm link chain. Use 4–5mm pearl connectors to attach the chains.

6 Use 4–5mm pearl connectors to attach an end link of each small-link chain to an end link of the large-link chain. Attach a pearl dangle to the same link.

7 Use a 6–7mm pearl connector to attach the other end link of the large-link chain and a lobster claw clasp. Use 4–5mm pearl connectors to attach the end links of the small-link chains to the 6–7mm pearl connector.

Pretty in paisley

These curvy links are the perfect place to nestle sparkling crystals

by Rebekah Gough

Simple wire wraps do the job nicely in this project, making it great for a novice wireworker. The unusual paisley chain adds dimension to the links.

SupplyList

bracelet 7½–8½ in. (19.1-21.6cm)
- **14–16** 4–6mm bicone crystals
- **35–40** in. (89–102cm) 26-gauge dead-soft wire
- 7–8 in. (18–20cm) paisley chain
- lobster claw clasp
- chainnose pliers
- roundnose pliers
- diagonal wire cutters

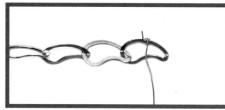

1 **a** Cut a 7–8-in. (18–20cm) piece of chain.
 b Cut a 2½-in. (6.4cm) piece of wire. Wrap the wire around one side of a link three times.

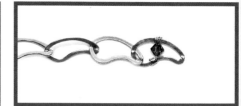

2 **a** String a bicone crystal on the wire. Wrap the wire around the other side of the link three times. Trim the excess wire. Use chainnose pliers to flatten the wire against the link.
 b Repeat steps 1b and 2a for each link.

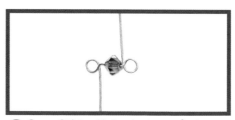

3 Cut a 2½-in. (6.4cm) piece of wire. Make the first half of a wrapped loop (Basics, p. 5). String a bicone and make the first half of a wrapped loop.

4 Attach the chain to one loop of the bicone unit and a lobster claw clasp to the other loop of the bicone unit. Complete the wraps.

Simply Stylish
Earrings

The

by Jane Konkel

Mixed-metal earrings — yesterday's fashion faux pas, today's clever accessory

Gone are the days when fashion dictated strictly silver or head-to-toe gold. For earrings to suit your every mood, go for mixed metals. Try a pair of wavy double rings, copper crescents, or mega-hoops on for size. What once was gauche now is good, so get in the mix.

mix is in

1 copper-crescent earrings • To make a dangle, string a 3mm cube bead on a head pin. Make a plain loop (Basics, p. 5) above the cube. Repeat with the remaining cubes.

2 Open a dangle's loop and attach it to the center loop of the crescent component. Close the loop. Attach the remaining dangles to every other bottom loop.

3 Cut six ½-in. (1.3cm) and two ⅜-in. (1cm) pieces of chain. Open two jump rings (Basics) and attach the shorter chains to the crescent's bottom outer loops. Close the jump rings. Use jump rings to attach the longer pieces of chain to the remaining bottom loops.

4 Cut a 2-in. (5cm) piece of chain. Using jump rings, attach each end to the crescent's top loops.

5 Use a jump ring to attach the center link to the loop of an earring wire. Make a second earring to match the first.

1 hoop earrings • Cut an 8-in. (20cm) piece of 20-gauge wire. Wrap the wire around a film canister or other round object. Remove the film canister. Cut an 8-in. (20cm) piece of 4mm gunmetal chain. Pass the wire through every other link of the chain. Center the chain on the wire.

2 Cut a 2¼-in. (5.7cm) piece of silver chain and a 1-in. (2.5cm) piece of 3mm gunmetal chain. Open a 4mm jump ring (Basics) and attach a charm to one chain. Close the jump ring. Repeat with the other charm and chain.

3 Bend the 20-gauge wire hoop approximately 1 in. (2.5cm) from each end to form a right angle.

Attach both chains to the horizontal wire. Wrap the horizontal wire around the vertical wire above the chains.

4 Make a wrapped loop with the vertical wire (Basics) and trim the excess.

5 Open a 5mm jump ring. Attach the dangle and the loop of an earring wire. Close the jump ring. Make a second earring to match the first.

1 double-ring earrings •
Cut a 1-in. (2.5cm) piece of gold chain. Open a gold jump ring (Basics) and attach an 11mm wavy silver jump ring and the chain. Close the jump ring.

Supply List

copper-crescent earrings
- **2** copper crescent-shaped components with 15-loop bottoms (Fire Mountain Gems, firemountaingems.com)
- **14** 3mm silver cube beads
- 1 ft. (30cm) silver chain, 2–3mm links
- **22** 3mm copper jump rings
- **14** 1-in. (2.5cm) decorative head pins
- pair of copper lever-back earring wires
- chainnose pliers
- roundnose pliers
- diagonal wire cutters

hoop earrings
- 16 in. (41cm) gunmetal cable chain, 4mm links
- 2 in. (5cm) gunmetal cable chain, 3mm links
- 5 in. (13cm) silver chain, 3mm links
- 16 in. (41cm) 20-gauge half-hard silver wire
- **4** 10–14mm silver charms in **2** shapes

- **2** 5mm silver jump rings
- **4** 4mm silver jump rings
- pair of silver earring wires
- chainnose pliers
- roundnose pliers
- diagonal wire cutters
- 35mm-film canister or other round object

double-ring earrings
- **4** 11mm wavy soldered jump rings, **2** silver and **2** gold (The Bead Shop, beadshop.com)
- **6** 5mm jump rings, **4** silver and **2** gold
- 3 in. (7.6cm) silver chain, 3–4mm links
- 3 in. (7.6cm) gold chain, 3–4mm links
- pair of decorative earring posts
- chainnose and roundnose pliers, or two pairs of chainnose pliers
- diagonal wire cutters

2 Cut a 1¾-in. (4.4cm) piece of silver chain. Open a silver jump ring and attach an 11mm wavy gold jump ring and the chain. Close the jump ring.

3 **a** Open a silver jump ring and attach both chains and the loop of an earring post. Close the jump ring.

b To make a second earring, cut a 1-in. (2.5cm) piece of silver chain and attach a wavy gold jump ring. Cut a 1¾-in. (4.4cm) piece of gold chain and attach a wavy silver jump ring. Repeat step 3a.

TIP
Although these earrings are made with two types of metals, you could add a third type. Try including gunmetal with the crescent pair, brushed silver with the hoops, or antiqued or oxidized metal with the double-ring pair.

Gypsy jewels

Crystals drift from chains in distinctive earrings

by Jane Konkel

Like an artist exploring different media, mix various materials, lengths, and color combinations as you create bohemian-style earrings. Incorporate leftover bits of chain into your clever creations, and reveal your inner artist.

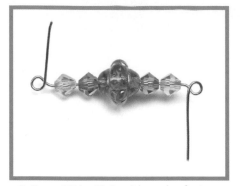

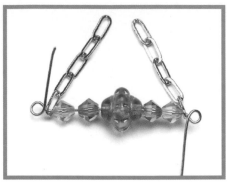

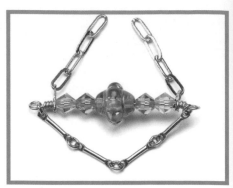

1 Cut a 2½-in. (6.4cm) length of wire. String two crystals, a saturn bead, and two crystals, alternating crystal colors. Make the first half of a wrapped loop on each end (Basics, p. 5).

2 Cut two ¾-in. (2cm) segments of fine chain. String one end link through one end of the wire, positioning it against the outside crystal. Repeat on the other end of the wire with the remaining piece of chain.

3 Cut a 1½-in. (3.8cm) segment of medium chain, making sure there is a round link in the center. Attach each end link of chain to a loop and complete the wraps.

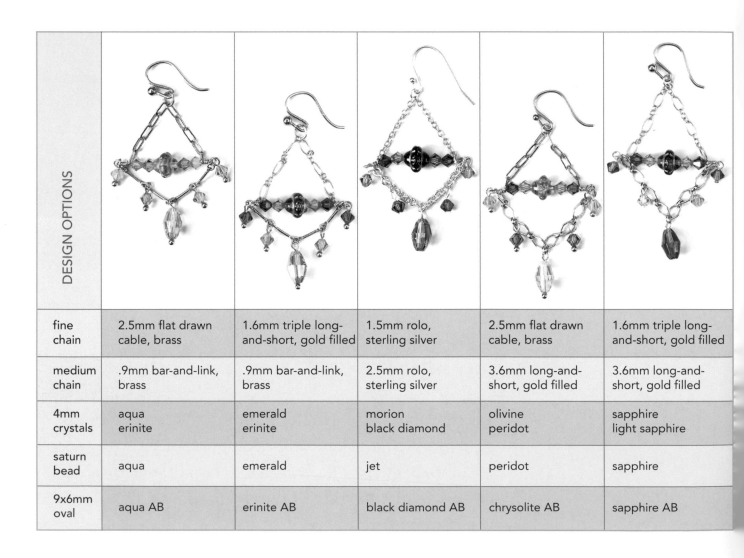

DESIGN OPTIONS					
fine chain	2.5mm flat drawn cable, brass	1.6mm triple long-and-short, gold filled	1.5mm rolo, sterling silver	2.5mm flat drawn cable, brass	1.6mm triple long-and-short, gold filled
medium chain	.9mm bar-and-link, brass	.9mm bar-and-link, brass	2.5mm rolo, sterling silver	3.6mm long-and-short, gold filled	3.6mm long-and-short, gold filled
4mm crystals	aqua erinite	emerald erinite	morion black diamond	olivine peridot	sapphire light sapphire
saturn bead	aqua	emerald	jet	peridot	sapphire
9x6mm oval	aqua AB	erinite AB	black diamond AB	chrysolite AB	sapphire AB

4 String an oval crystal on a decorative head pin. Make a plain loop (Basics) above the crystal. Make four more dangles with bicone crystals.

5 Open the loop of the oval dangle and attach it to the center link on the lower chain. Close the loop. Attach the remaining bicone dangles to the lower chain, alternating colors.

Supply List

earrings

- **2** 9 x 6mm oval crystals
- **2** 8mm Czech glass saturn beads (Rio Grande, riogrande.com)
- **16** 4mm bicone crystals, **8** each of **2** colors
- 5 in. (13cm) 24-gauge wire
- 4 in. (10cm) each of **2** chains, **1** fine and **1** medium
- **10** 1½-in. (3.8cm) plain or decorative head pins
- **2–4** 4mm jump rings
- pair of earring wires
- chainnose pliers
- roundnose pliers
- diagonal wire cutters

TIP
For earrings that hang perpendicular to your ear lobe, rather than parallel, attach a second jump ring to the first.

6 Open a jump ring (Basics) and string each end link of the upper chain. Close the jump ring.

7 Open an earring wire. String the jump ring. Close the loop. Make a second earring to match the first.

Modern
metal earrings

Chain, links, and jump rings give these easy earrings a modern edge

by Gretta Van Someren

Mixed or matched, metal chains make a stylish statement. You can combine different metal finishes or keep it simple with a single type. Use longer chains for earrings with more movement.

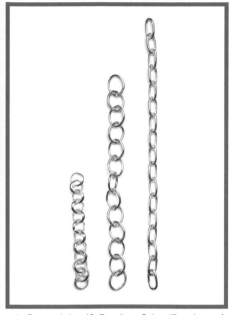

Supply List

earrings
- **2** 10–20mm charms or drops
- **2** 10–12mm links, washers, or soldered jump rings
- **1** ft. (30cm) chain, 4–6mm links, in three styles
- **2** 8–9mm jump rings
- **6** 4–5mm jump rings
- pair of lever-back earring wires
- chainnose and roundnose pliers, or **2** pairs of chainnose pliers
- diagonal wire cutters

1 Cut a 1-in. (2.5cm), a 2-in. (5cm), and a 2¼-in. (5.7cm) piece of chain, each in a different style.

2 Open a 4–5mm jump ring (Basics, p. 5). Attach a charm or drop and the 1-in. (2.5cm) piece of chain. Close the jump ring.

3 Use a 4–5mm jump ring to attach all three chains. Use an 8–9mm jump ring to attach the 4–5mm jump ring and a link.

4 Use a 4–5mm jump ring to attach the 8–9mm jump ring and the loop of an earring wire. Make a second earring the mirror image of the first.

TIPS
- If you like your metals dark, use liver of sulfur to oxidize the chain and findings.
- You can either look for individual links, washers, or soldered jump rings or cut a few links of chain left over from previous projects.

by Brenda Schweder

It's a

1 Cut pairs of chain segments in assorted lengths for each connector bar's hanging loop. (These range from 1¼ to 2¾ in./ 32 to 70mm.) Reserve one segment from each pair for the second earring.

2 Open a jump ring (Basics, p. 5) and link it to a connector loop. String groupings of three or more chain segments on each jump ring; close the jump rings.

3 String beads on head pins as desired and make the first half of a wrapped loop (Basics).

4 For top-drilled beads, cut a 2½-in. (64mm) piece of wire. String a bead and make a set of wraps above it (Basics).

Make the first half of a wrapped loop ⅛ in. (3mm) above the wraps.

breeze

Whip up cascade earrings in a flurry of seasonal colors

Designing is a breeze when you attach all the chain segments first, then arrange the placement of gemstones and crystals on this curtain of chain. Try summery watercolors in peridot, aquamarine, and tanzanite or muted fall hues of garnet, carnelian, and berry quartz.

5 Attach dangles as desired, staggering their placement along each chain segment. Complete the wraps as you go.

6 Open the loop of an earring wire and attach the top loop of the connector bar. Close the earring wire loop.

Make a second earring in the mirror image of the first, using the remaining chain segments.

Supply List

earrings
- 3–8 ft. (.91-2.44m) cable or figure-8 chain, approx. 2mm
- assorted gemstones and crystals, 3–12mm
- **2** connector bars
- 1½-in. (38mm) plain or decorative head pins
- 24-gauge wire, half hard
- 3–4mm jump rings
- pair of earring wires
- chainnose pliers
- roundnose pliers
- diagonal wire cutters

Aquamarine earrings

by Jane Konkel

Catch a metal fish bead on a length of chain

Because one strand of aquamarine rondelles is enough to make several pairs of these earrings, you may want to make an extra set to pass on to a Pisces friend.

1 earrings • On a decorative head pin, string: fish-shaped bead, two rondelles, spacer, rondelle. Make the first half of a wrapped loop (Basics, p. 5). Cut a 1-in. (2.5cm) piece of chain. Attach the loop of the fish-bead unit to one end of the chain. Complete the wraps.

2 On a decorative head pin, string one or two rondelles. Make the first half of a wrapped loop. Make three bead units.

3 Attach the loop of each bead unit to a link of chain as shown. Complete the wraps.

4 Open the loop of an earring wire (Basics). Attach the dangle and close the loop. Make a second earring to match the first.

Simply Stylish

Jewelry sets

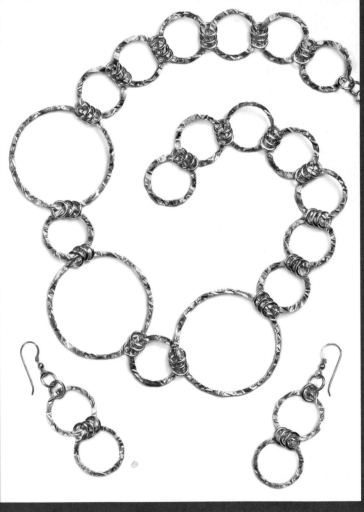

Real Venetian beads

string true

Spectacular beads go a long way when paired with distinctive chain

by Cathy Jakicic

There are any number of "Venetian-style" beads available. But just as no one would mistake the "Venice" built in a Las Vegas hotel for the romantic Italian city, imitation beads don't compare to those made by the actual artisans of Venice and Murano, Italy. Real Venetian beads can be made with 24k gold or .999 silver foil, gold leaf, or copper flakes. They are crafted by hand, using secret glass recipes and traditional techniques passed down through generations.

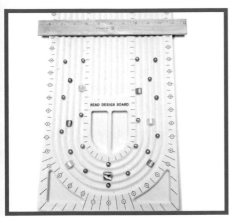

1 necklace • Decide how long you want your necklace strands to be. Mark the lengths on a bead design board and arrange Venetian beads in the channels.

2 Cut a 2-in. (5cm) piece of wire. Make the first half of a wrapped loop (Basics, p. 5). String a bead and make the first half of a wrapped loop. Put the bead unit back on the board. Repeat with the remaining beads.

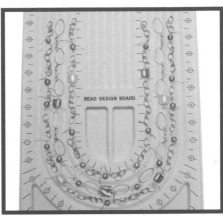

3 Measure the spaces between the bead units. Cut chain pieces to those lengths, and position them on the board. Use cable chain for the longest and shortest strands. Use long-and-short–link chain for the middle strand.

4 Attach the chains and bead units without completing the wraps. Check the fit, allowing 3 in. (7.6cm) for finishing. Add or remove bead units or chain, if necessary.

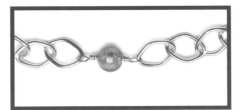

5 Complete the wraps on the bead units.

6 Trim one link from the cable chain to use as half of the clasp, and two 22mm links from the long-and-short–link chain to use as jump rings. Carefully cut the top of a 22mm link and open it like a jump ring (Basics). Use it to attach one end of each strand and an S-hook clasp. Repeat on the other end, substituting the cable-chain link for the S-hook clasp.

TIP
Don't be afraid to mix and match beads made with different techniques.
This necklace uses:
• 15mm window flat square in amber and white
• 11mm flat foil squares in amber
• 10mm crystal matte cubes in amber
• 8mm round foil beads in aqua and blue

1 **earrings** • On a head pin, string a Venetian bead. Make the first half of a wrapped loop (Basics).

2 Cut a piece of chain with one long and three short links. Attach the bead unit to the long link. Complete the wraps.

3 Open the loop of an earring wire (Basics). Attach the dangle and close the loop. Make a second earring to match the first.

DESIGN ALTERNATIVE

Saving your money for travel? Keep the necklace to one strand, being sure to use subtle but stunning blown-glass beads with a delicate, large-link chain.

SupplyList

necklace: strands are 29 in. (74cm), 27 in. (69cm), and 26 in. (66cm)
- **25–29** assorted Venetian beads
- **50–60 in.** (1.3–1.5m) 22-gauge half-hard wire
- **38–46 in.** (.97–1.2m) cable chain, 12mm links
- **20–24 in.** (51–61cm) long-and-short-link chain, 11mm and 22mm links
- S-hook clasp
- chainnose pliers
- roundnose pliers
- diagonal wire cutters
- bead design board

earrings
- **2** 8mm Venetian beads
- **4 in.** (10cm) long-and-short-link chain, 11mm and 22mm links
- **2** 1½-in. (3.8cm) head pins
- pair of earring wires
- chainnose pliers
- roundnose pliers
- diagonal wire cutters

Printed
portals

Sample a
parade
of pendants

by Nina Cooper

This necklace features a cascade of round pendants handmade from Bali silver. The pendants provide a glimpse of Japanese plum blossoms and flowery English poetry, Chinese text and a swirling pool.

1 necklace • Cut a 20–24-in. (51–61cm) piece of silk cord. Center: 24mm pendant, three or four spacers, 40mm pendant, three or four spacers, 24mm pendant.

2 On each end, string three or four spacers, an 18mm pendant, three or four spacers, and a 12mm pendant.

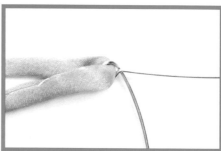

3 Cut a 4-in. (10cm) piece of wire. Make the first half of a wrapped loop (Basics, p. 5) 1 in. (2.5cm) from one end. String one end of the cord and fold it, leaving a ½-in. (1.3cm) tail. Complete the wraps, wrapping the wire tightly around the folded cord. Trim the excess wire and tuck the end under the wraps. Repeat on the other end of the cord. Trim the excess cord.

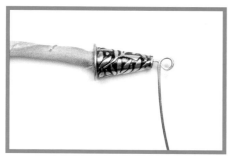

4 On each end, string a cone and make the first half of a wrapped loop.

5 On each end, attach half of a clasp and complete the wraps.

TIP
If you are layering pendants, it helps to alternate between busy and simple patterns.

DESIGN ALTERNATIVE

For a budget-friendly necklace, use just three small silver pendants, or hang brass pendants from leather cord. Brass pendants from Jewels n Findings, jewelsnfindings.com.

Supply List

Supplies from Nina Designs, ninadesigns.com. All pendants have jump rings attached.

necklace 16 in. (41cm)
- 40mm extra-large disk pendant
- 2 24mm round domed pendants
- 2 18mm round domed pendants
- 2 12mm round domed pendants
- 18–24 9mm large-hole flat spacers
- 20–24 in. (51–61cm) silk cord, 3mm wide
- 8 in. (20cm) 22-gauge dead-soft wire
- 2 13mm small cones
- toggle clasp
- chainnose pliers
- roundnose pliers
- diagonal wire cutters

earrings
- 2 12mm oval beads
- 2 9mm large-hole flat spacers
- 2 2-in. (5cm) decorative head pins
- 2 5mm jump rings
- pair of decorative earring wires to match oval beads
- chainnose pliers
- roundnose pliers
- diagonal wire cutters

1 earrings • On a decorative head pin, string an oval bead and make the first half of a wrapped loop (Basics).

2 Attach a spacer and complete the wraps.

3 Open a jump ring (Basics) and attach the dangle and the loop of an earring wire. Close the jump ring. Make a second earring to match the first.

Create a coo

patina

Patinated copper puts a necklace, bracelet, and earrings in blue mode

by Jane Konkel

Make an easy necklace by stringing a strand of beads through cool-blue chain. Suspending copper chain over ammonia turns it a rich shade of blue. Pass a short strand through the chain for a matching bracelet, and use patinated findings to make chandelier earrings.

SupplyList

necklace 16 in. (41cm)
- 8-in. (20cm) strand 9mm cathedral fire-polished crystals
- 16-in. (41cm) strand 6–8mm pearls
- **42–54** 3mm faceted round spacers
- flexible beading wire, .014 or .015
- 16–20 in. (41–51cm) copper chain, 20mm links (Midwest Beads, midwestbeads.biz)
- **2** crimp beads
- S-hook clasp with **2** jump rings
- chainnose pliers
- roundnose pliers
- crimping pliers (optional)
- diagonal wire cutters

bracelet 6½–8½ in. (16.5–19.1cm)
- **3–4** 9mm cathedral fire-polished crystals
- **12–15** 6–8mm pearls
- **16–20** 3mm faceted round spacers
- flexible beading wire, .014 or .015
- 6–8 in. (15–20cm) copper chain, 20mm links (Midwest Beads)
- **2–4** 5–6mm jump rings (optional)
- **2** crimp beads
- S-hook clasp with **2** jump rings
- chainnose pliers
- roundnose pliers
- crimping pliers (optional)
- diagonal wire cutters

earrings
- **2** 9mm cathedral fire-polished crystals
- **4** 6–8mm pearls
- **6** 3mm faceted round spacers
- pair of 40mm copper chandelier findings
- **6** 2-in. (5cm) head pins
- pair of earring wires
- chainnose pliers
- roundnose pliers
- diagonal wire cutters

1 necklace • Cut a piece of beading wire (Basics, p. 5). On the wire, string: pearl, spacer, pearl, spacer, pearl, spacer, crystal. Repeat until the strand is within 2 in. (5cm) of the finished length.

2 Cut a piece of chain to the length you want your necklace to be. Prepare the chain (see "Patinating," p. 60). Pass the strand down through one link and up through the next until you've strung the entire chain.

3 On each end of the beaded strand, string a spacer, a crimp bead, a spacer, and a jump ring (to attach to an S-hook clasp). Check the fit, and add or remove beads if necessary. Go back through the beads just strung and tighten the wire. Crimp the crimp bead (Basics) and trim the excess wire.

4 On each end, open the jump ring (Basics) and attach the chain. Close the jump ring.

bracelet • Follow steps 1–4 of the necklace. To adjust the length of your bracelet, attach additional jump rings to one end.

1 **earrings** • On a head pin, string a crystal and a spacer. Make the first half of a wrapped loop (Basics). Repeat to make two pearl units.

2 Prepare two chandelier findings (see "Patinating," below). Attach the crystal unit to the center loop of a chandelier finding. Attach each pearl unit to an outer loop. Complete the wraps.

3 Open the loop of an earring wire (Basics). Attach the dangle and close the loop. Make a second earring to match the first.

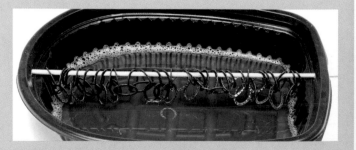

PATINATING

To add a blue patina to copper:
1) Soak copper pieces in a saltwater solution (approximately 2 tbsp. salt per 4 oz. water) for four to eight hours.
2) Hang the copper pieces from a dowel that you've cut to fit the rim of a plastic container.

3) Fill the bottom of the container with ½ in. (1.3cm) of ammonia.
4) Cover with a tight-fitting lid and set aside for four to ten hours.
5) In a ventilated area, spray dry pieces with a protective matte finish, such as Krylon (available at craft or hardware stores).

Quick
silver

Complex shapes add drama
to a simple design

by Carol McKinney

SupplyList

necklace 17 in. (43cm)
- **9–13** 13–17mm hollow Karen Hill Tribe silver nuggets, in assorted shapes (Rings & Things, rings-things.com)
- **16-in. (41cm)** strand 13–15mm oval beads
- **12–16** 9mm silver nuggets
- flexible beading wire, .014 or .015
- **2** crimp beads
- toggle clasp
- chainnose or crimping pliers
- diagonal wire cutters

long earrings
- **4** 13–15mm oval beads
- **2** 13mm hollow rectangular Karen Hill Tribe silver nuggets (Rings & Things, rings-things.com)
- **2** 2½-in. (6.4cm) head pins
- pair of earring wires
- chainnose pliers
- roundnose pliers
- diagonal wire cutters

short earrings
- **2** 13–15mm oval beads
- **4** 9mm silver nuggets (Rings & Things, rings-things.com)
- **2** 2½-in. (6.4cm) head pins
- pair of earring wires
- chainnose pliers
- roundnose pliers
- diagonal wire cutters

The design is timeless and the stringing takes no time at all. What could be better? Just let these irregularly shaped silver nuggets take center stage, add gemstones (turquoise is silver's best friend) or ceramic ovals, and you're done. The matching earring options are a snap, too.

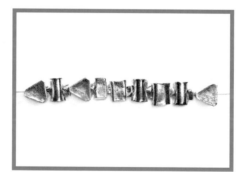

1 **necklace** • Cut a piece of beading wire (Basics, p. 5). Center a 4-in. (10cm) section of silver beads, alternating between 13–17mm nuggets and 9mm nuggets. End with a 13–17mm nugget.

2 On each end, string oval beads until the necklace is within 1 in. (2.5cm) of the finished length. String two or three 9mm nuggets, a crimp bead, and half of a clasp. Check the fit and add or remove beads if necessary. Go back through the beads just strung and tighten the wire. Crimp the crimp bead (Basics) and trim the excess wire.

TIPS
- Arrange the different shapes of the larger silver nuggets in the desired order before you string them.
- If you like, attach a decorative oval bead to the loop half of the clasp.

1 **long earrings** • On a head pin, string an oval bead, a 13mm nugget, and an oval bead. Make a plain loop (Basics).

2 Open the loop of an earring wire (Basics). Attach the dangle and close the loop. Make a second earring to match the first.

1 **short earrings** • On a head pin, string a 9mm nugget, an oval bead, and a nugget. Make a wrapped loop (Basics).

2 Open the loop of an earring wire (Basics). Attach the dangle and close the loop. Make a second earring to match the first.

DESIGN ALTERNATIVE

Create strong visual impact with dramatic black beads and a few silver beads placed off-center.

Angular chain balances gemstones in
a necklace-and-earring set

by Brenda Schweder

Create an elegant drape with beads and chain

For a unified design, select rectangular gemstones that have a rich pattern. Then, find chains that accentuate the pattern. Figaro or curb chains, with their angular links, also complement the beads' shapes.

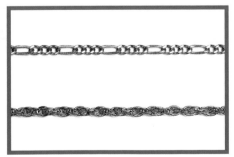

1 necklace • For the shortest strand: Determine the finished length of your necklace. Subtract 1 in. (2.5cm) and cut a piece of 6–8mm-link chain to that length. (The shortest strands shown here are 14½ in./36.8cm.) For the middle strand, cut a piece of 4–5mm-link chain 1½–2 in. (3.8–5cm) longer than the previous piece.

2 For the longest strand, cut a 15-in. (38cm) piece of beading wire. String a spacer, an accent bead, and a spacer.

TIP
Consider using vintage or base-metal chain, both of which have patinas that echo darker gemstone patterns.

3 a On one end, string an alternating pattern of four rectangular beads and four spacers.

b On the other end, string an alternating pattern of six rectangular beads and six spacers.

4 Cut two 5–7-in. (13–18cm) pieces of 4–5mm-link chain.

On each end of the wire, string a crimp bead and one chain. Go back through the last few beads strung and tighten the wire. Crimp the crimp bead (Basics, p. 5) and trim the excess wire.

5 Using chainnose pliers, close a crimp cover over each crimp bead.

6 Check the fit, allowing 1 in. (2.5cm) for finishing. Trim chain, if necessary. On each end, open a 4–5mm jump ring (Basics). Attach one end of each chain and a soldered jump ring. Close the jump ring.

On one end, attach an S-hook clasp. Close half of the S with chainnose pliers.

1 **earrings** • On a decorative head pin, string a rectangular bead. Make a plain or wrapped loop (Basics).

2 Cut a 1½-in. (3.8cm) piece of 4–5mm-link chain and a 1¾-in. (4.4cm) piece of 6–8mm-link chain. Open the loop of an earring wire (Basics). Attach the bead unit and each chain. Close the loop. Make a second earring to match the first.

Supply List

necklace: longest strand 18–22 in. (46–56cm)
- 24–30mm accent bead
- 16-in. (41cm) strand rectangular beads, approximately 8 x 16mm
- **12** 3–4mm flat spacers
- flexible beading wire, .014 or .015
- 14–17 in. (36–43cm) chain, 6–8mm links
- 24–32 in. (61–81cm) chain, 4–5mm links
- **2** 4–5mm jump rings
- **2** crimp beads
- **2** crimp covers
- S-hook clasp with **2** soldered jump rings
- chainnose and roundnose pliers, or **2** pairs of chainnose pliers
- diagonal wire cutters
- crimping pliers (optional)

earrings
- **2** rectangular beads, approximately 8 x 16mm, left over from necklace
- 4 in. (10cm) chain, 6–8mm links
- 3½ in. (8.9cm) chain, 4–5mm links
- **2** 2-in. (5cm) decorative head pins
- pair of earring wires
- chainnose pliers
- roundnose pliers
- diagonal wire cutters

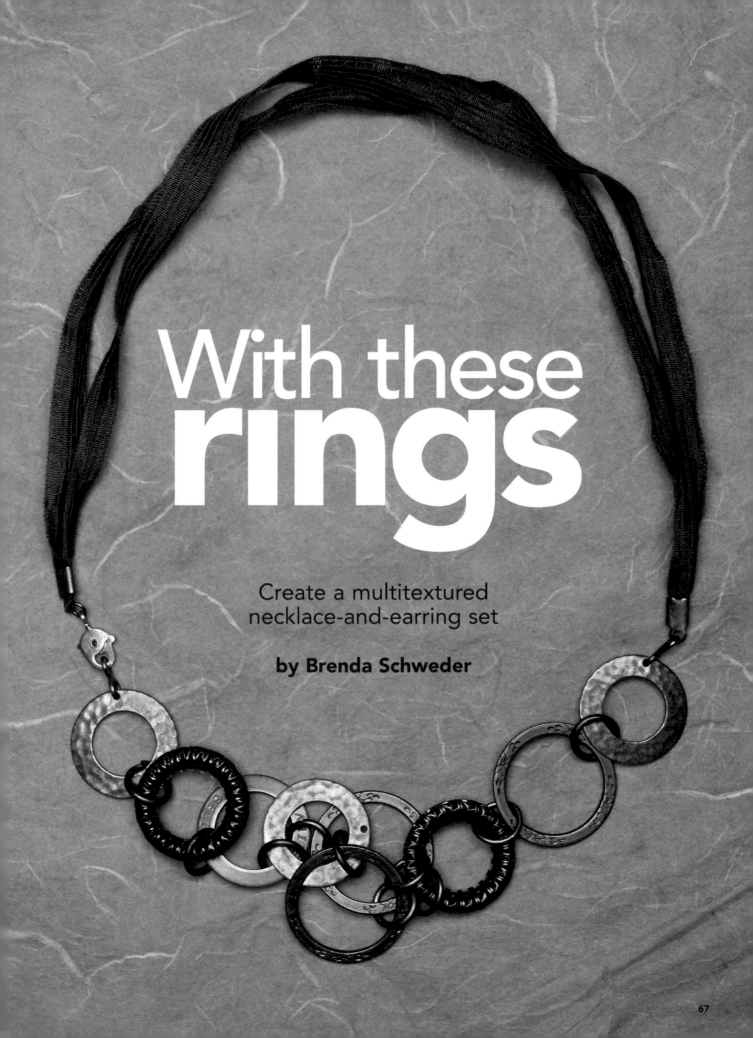

With these rings

Create a multitextured
necklace-and-earring set

by **Brenda Schweder**

When I saw these different rings, I knew they were meant to be together. The textures play off each other beautifully, and the softness of the ribbon feels as good as it looks. I loved the front-hooking clasp so much, I used it again in matching earrings.

1 necklace • Open 10 10–15mm jump rings (Basics, p. 5). Attach two hammered rings, two filigree rings, two "believe" rings, and three "garden" rings as shown. Close the jump rings as you go.

2 Open a loop of a figure-8 connector. Attach one end of the ring section and close the loop. Repeat on the other end.

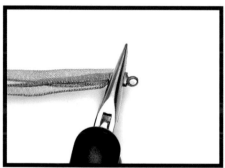

3 Decide how long you want your necklace to be. Subtract the length of the ring section and cut a piece of ribbon twice that length. Fold the ribbon in half lengthwise. Apply glue to one end and fold the ribbon widthwise, then attach a crimp end (Basics). Repeat on the other end.

4 Use a 4–6mm jump ring to attach a crimp end and a clasp.

5 Open a loop of the figure-8 connector on the remaining end of the ring section. Attach the remaining crimp end and close the loop.

Supply List

All components from Vintaj Natural Brass Co., vintaj.com.

necklace 18 in. (46cm)
- **3** 25mm "garden" rings
- **2** 24mm filigree rings
- **2** 23mm "believe" rings
- **2** 22mm hammered rings
- 24–26 in. (61–66cm) 8mm ribbon
- **10** 10–15mm jump rings
- **4**–6mm jump ring
- **2** 9mm figure-8 connectors
- **2** 9mm crimp ends
- lobster claw clasp
- chainnose and roundnose pliers, or **2** pairs of chainnose pliers
- E6000 adhesive

earrings
- **2** 22mm hammered rings
- **4** 4–6mm jump rings
- **2** lobster claw clasps
- pair of lever-back earring wires
- chainnose and roundnose pliers, or **2** pairs of chainnose pliers

TIP
Choose your jump ring sizes based on how much movement you want the ring section to have. Larger jump rings will give the piece more flow; smaller jump rings offer more stability.

1 **earrings** • Open a jump ring (Basics). Attach a hammered ring and a clasp. Close the jump ring.

2 Use a jump ring to attach an earring wire and the dangle. Make a second earring to match the first.

DESIGN ALTERNATIVE
Use crystal-ring pendants for a dressed-up, night-on-the-town look.

Spoon style, baby

Turn silverware into silver-worn jewelry

by Jane Konkel

Found objects (like baby spoons or travel souvenirs) make unique focal components. Spoons with engraved designs, dates, or names are fabulous finds. Repurpose one as a key chain for a new dad, or hang a spoon pendant-style from a chain. For a cuff with character, drill, bend, and hammer the spoon.

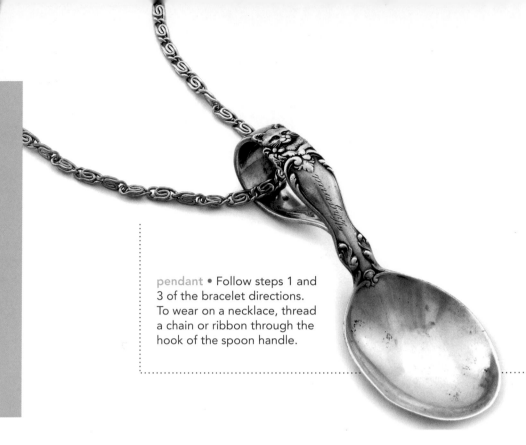

SupplyList

both projects
- vintage spoon
- polishing cloth

bracelet
- 1½–3½ in. (3.8–8.9cm) chain, 12–18mm links
- **2–3** 12–14mm oval jump rings
- large lobster claw clasp
- chainnose and roundnose pliers, or **2** pairs chainnose pliers
- diagonal wire cutters
- bracelet mandrel
- rawhide hammer
- steel hole punch or drill

pendant
- chainnose pliers

pendant • Follow steps 1 and 3 of the bracelet directions. To wear on a necklace, thread a chain or ribbon through the hook of the spoon handle.

1 bracelet • Use a polishing cloth to remove some of the tarnish from a spoon.

2 Use a steel hole punch or drill to bore a hole through the bowl of the spoon. The hole should be about ¼ in. (6mm) from the edge.

3 Position your chainnose pliers about ¾ in. (1.9cm) from the handle's end. Bend the handle around the pliers to make a hook.

4 On a bracelet mandrel, hammer the spoon to fit around your wrist. Slightly flatten the bowl of the spoon.

5 Open a jump ring (Basics, p. 5) or a chain link and attach the spoon's hook. Attach a second jump ring or chain link to the first.

6 Decide how long you want your bracelet to be. Subtract the length of the spoon and cut a piece of chain to that length. Attach a lobster claw clasp to one end. Attach the spoon's hole and the other end of the chain.

Chain

Layer cable and rope chains in a chunky necklace and bracelet

by Brenda Schweder

TIP
Since the largest chain (13 x 21mm links) is the least variable in length, determine the finished length and cut that piece first.

maker

A trio of chains in different sizes, shapes, and finishes combines with a sprinkling of spacers for an extra-long necklace or multitextured bracelet. Make one or both, and no matter how the winds of fashion blow, you'll be covered.

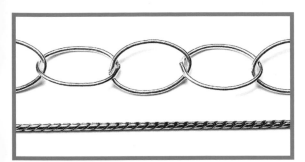

1 necklace • Determine the finished length of your necklace. Cut a piece of large cable chain to that length. Subtract 1 in. (2.5cm) and cut a piece of rope chain to that length.

2 Cut a piece of small cable chain 1½ in. (3.8cm) longer than the large cable chain. Center a pendant on the small cable chain.

3 Check the fit, allowing 1 in. (2.5cm) for finishing, and trim links from each chain if necessary. Open a jump ring (Basics, p. 5) and attach all three chains. Close the jump ring. Open another jump ring and attach the previous jump ring and half of a clasp. Close the jump ring. Repeat on the other end.

4 Use jump rings to attach spacers to the cable chains, as desired.

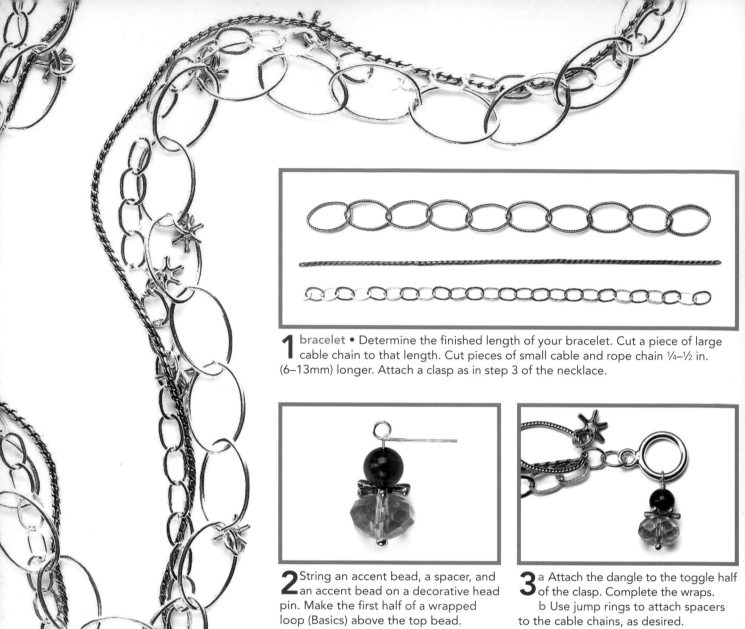

1 bracelet • Determine the finished length of your bracelet. Cut a piece of large cable chain to that length. Cut pieces of small cable and rope chain ¼–½ in. (6–13mm) longer. Attach a clasp as in step 3 of the necklace.

2 String an accent bead, a spacer, and an accent bead on a decorative head pin. Make the first half of a wrapped loop (Basics) above the top bead.

3 a Attach the dangle to the toggle half of the clasp. Complete the wraps.
b Use jump rings to attach spacers to the cable chains, as desired.

Supply List

necklace 24½ in. (62cm)
• pendant, with bail to accommodate small cable chain
• 2–3 ft. (61–91cm) large cable chain, 13 x 21mm links (Silver City, silvercityonline.com)
• 2–3 ft. (61–91cm) small cable chain, 5 x 7mm links
• 2–3 ft. (61–91cm) rope chain, 2mm diameter
• **15–20** 8mm flat spacers (Kamol Beads, info@kamol.com)
• **19–24** 5mm jump rings
• toggle clasp
• chainnose pliers
• roundnose pliers
• diagonal wire cutters

bracelet
• 6–8 in. (15–20cm) large cable chain, 13 x 21mm links
• 6–8 in. (15–20cm) small cable chain, 5 x 7mm links
• 6–8 in. (15–20cm) rope chain, 2mm diameter
• **2** 6–10mm accent beads
• 2-in. (5cm) decorative head pin
• **7–12** 8mm flat spacers
• **11–16** 5mm jump rings
• toggle clasp
• chainnose pliers
• roundnose pliers
• diagonal wire cutters

Balanced
drape

Chandelier
components give
a necklace and
bracelet a flexible
design

by Lauren M. Hadley

To make a shimmering necklace that drapes gracefully, start with decorative chandelier components, then pick chain and gemstones that work with the components' style. I like pale, ethereal labradorite or pink Peruvian opal as options. In the bracelet, using only two gemstones will keep the focus on the ornate components.

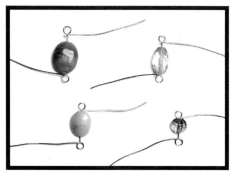

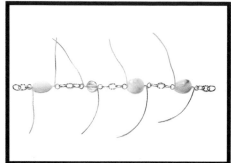

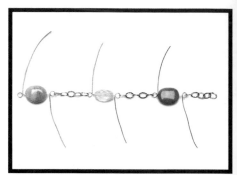

1 **necklace •** Cut a 3½-in. (7.6cm) piece of wire. Make the first half of a wrapped loop (Basics, p. 5). String a 13–16mm (large) bead and make the first half of a wrapped loop. Make three large-bead units. Make two 10–12mm (medium) bead units, 14 8–9mm (small) bead units, and six round-bead units.

2 To make the first (longest) strand: Cut nine ½-in. (1.3cm) pieces of 3–4mm (small) cable chain. Center a piece of chain. On each end, attach: small-bead unit, chain, round-bead unit, chain, small-bead unit, chain, small-bead unit, chain. Complete the wraps as you go.

To make the fifth (shortest) strand: Cut seven ½-in. (1.3cm) pieces of small chain. Attach bead units as in the first strand, omitting the chain on each end. Leave the end loops unwrapped.

3 To make the third strand: Cut six ¾-in. (1.9cm) pieces of small chain. Center a large-bead unit. On each end, attach: chain, medium-bead unit, chain, large-bead unit, chain. Complete the wraps as you go.

To make the second and fourth strands: Cut two pieces of small chain (the strands in this necklace are 8 and 7½ in./20 and 19.1cm).

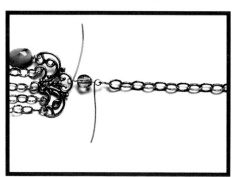

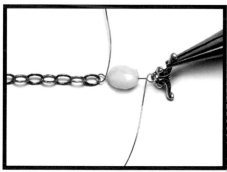

4 Open a jump ring (Basics). Attach one end of the first strand and an end loop of a five-to-one component. Close the jump ring. Repeat on the other end. Use jump rings to attach the second, third, and fourth strands and the corresponding loops of the component. Connect the open wraps on each end of the fifth strand with the corresponding loops of the component. Complete the wraps.

5 Decide how long you want your necklace to be, subtract the length of the beaded section, and cut a piece of 5–6mm (large) cable chain to that length. Cut the chain in half. Use a round-bead unit to attach the remaining loop of one component and a chain. Complete the wraps. Repeat on the other side.

6 Check the fit, allowing 1 in. (2.5cm) for finishing, and trim chain from each end if necessary. On each end, use a small-bead unit to attach half of a clasp.

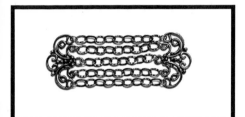

1 **bracelet •** Cut five 1¼–1¾ in. (3.2–4.4cm) pieces of chain. Open a jump ring (Basics). Attach a chain and a loop of a five-to-one component and close the jump ring. Use a jump ring to attach each end of each chain and the corresponding loop of the component.

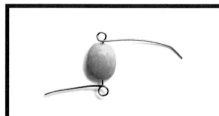

2 Cut a 3-in. (7.6cm) piece of wire. Make the first half of a wrapped loop (Basics). String an 8–9mm bead and make the first half of a wrapped loop. Make two bead units.

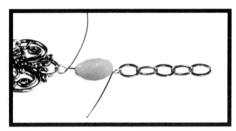

3 Cut two 1–1½-in. (2.5–3.8cm) pieces of chain. Attach one loop of a bead unit and the remaining loop of a five-to-one component and a chain. Complete the wraps.

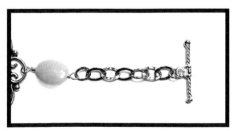

4 Check the fit, allowing 1 in. (2.5cm) for finishing. Trim chain if necessary. On each end, use a jump ring to attach half of a clasp and the chain.

DESIGN ALTERNATIVE

Make earrings using three-to-one (instead of five-to-one) components. The smaller scale won't overpower the necklace and bracelet.

SupplyList

labradorite necklace 20 in. (51cm); pink opal 21½ in. (54.6cm)
- **3** 13–16mm beads
- **2** 10–12mm beads
- **14** 8–9mm beads
- **6** 6mm round beads
- **75** in. (1.9m) 24-gauge half-hard wire
- **8–12** in. (20–30cm) cable chain, 5–6mm links
- **30–35** in. (76–89cm) cable chain, 3–4mm links
- **2** five-to-one chandelier components
- **10** 4mm jump rings
- toggle clasp
- chainnose pliers
- roundnose pliers
- diagonal wire cutters

bracelet 6½–7½ in. (16.5–19.1cm)
- **2** 8–9mm beads
- **6** in. (15cm) 24-gauge half-hard wire
- **10–12** in. (25–30cm) cable chain, 5–6mm links
- **2** five-to-one chandelier components
- **12** 4mm jump rings
- toggle clasp
- chainnose pliers
- roundnose pliers
- diagonal wire cutters

TIPS
- For an economical alternative, use a graduated strand of 8–16mm beads.
- Try jasper or another gemstone that shows a range of colors.

Copper concept

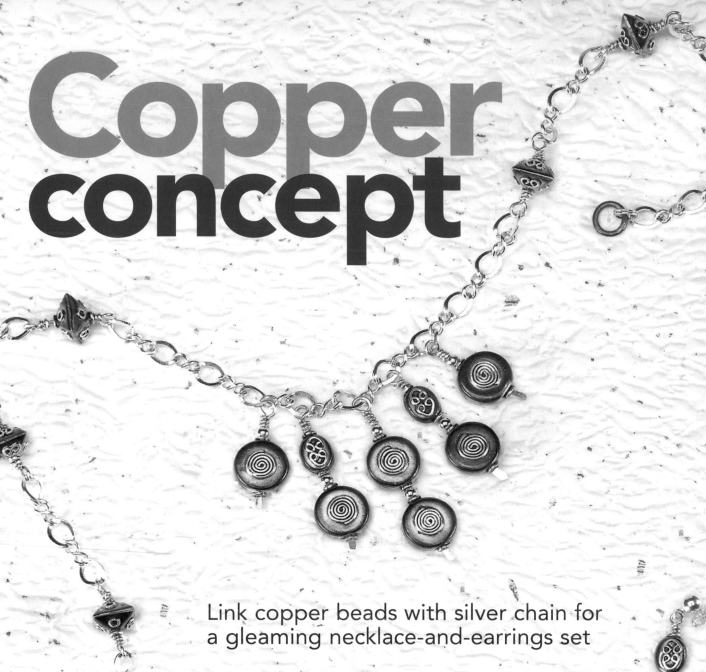

Link copper beads with silver chain for a gleaming necklace-and-earrings set

by Linda J. Augsburg

Copper and pewter make an eye-catching combination in this necklace-and-earrings set. The contasting colors play well into the mixed-metals style, and the beads balance easily on lengths of chain.

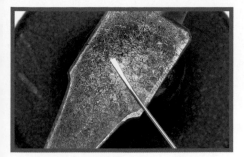

1 necklace • Cut five 2½-in. (6cm) lengths of 20-gauge wire. Using an anvil or bench block and hammer, flatten one end of each piece of wire to form a paddle-shaped head pin.

2 String the copper and 2.5mm round beads on head pins as shown above. Make the first half of a wrapped loop (Basics, p. 5) above the end bead on each head pin.

Supply**List**

both projects
• 38½ in. (0.95m) 20-gauge wire
• 14 in. (36cm) figure-8 chain
• anvil or bench block
• hammer

necklace 23 in. (58cm)
• 14 9–14mm copper and pewter beads, 6 each of 2 styles and 2 in a third style
• 6 2.5mm round beads
• 24mm copper and silver S-clasp with soldered jump rings
• 2 5mm split rings
• chainnose pliers
• roundnose pliers
• diagonal wire cutters
• split ring pliers (optional)

earrings
• 9–14mm copper and pewter beads
• pair of earring posts with loop

3 To make the connecting units, cut six 2-in. (5cm) pieces of wire and center a bead on each one. Bend each wire end into a right angle pointing in opposite directions. Make the bends 1⁄16 in. (2mm) from each end of the bead.

Cut four 1¼-in. (3cm) lengths of chain for the necklace sides. Cut a 5-in. (13cm) length of chain for the front. Set the rest of the chain aside.

4 Attach the dangles to the front chain as shown and complete the wrapped loops (Basics).

1 earrings • Make two 1½-in. (4cm) long paddle-shaped head pins as in step 1 of the necklace. String a bead on each. Make the first half of a wrapped loop at the unfinished end of each head pin.

5 Make the first part of a wrapped loop on each side of the connecting units. Slide one end of a unit through the end link on the front chain section. Slide the other end through the end link on a side chain section. Complete the wrapped loops.

Join another unit and side chain section to this end of the necklace. Then add one more unit to the end link of chain. Complete the wrapped loop on all but the last connector unit.

Repeat this step on the opposite end of the front section.

6 Check the length of the necklace. Cut two 1¼-in. or longer lengths of chain. Attach one chain to each unfinished connecting unit. Complete the wrapped loops.

To attach the clasp, use split rings to connect each soldered jump ring to an end chain link.

2 Cut two 2-in. long pieces of wire. String a bead on each and make the first half of a wrapped loop at both ends.

3 Cut a ¾-in. (2cm) length of chain. Slide the head pin onto the end link. Slide a bead unit onto the link at the opposite end. Complete the wrapped loops. Open the loop on the earring finding and attach the wrapped loop to the finding. Make a second earring to match the first.

Moving in fashionable circles

by Heidi Hermreck

Join different-sized silver and gold hoops with jump rings

These hoops have an eye-catching hammered texture that needs no embellishment. If you want a touch of color, add bead dangles to a pair of earrings to bring this fashion-forward look full circle.

1 necklace • Open a gold jump ring (Basics, p. 5). Attach a silver hoop and a gold hoop. Close the jump ring. Attach a silver jump ring on each side of the gold jump ring.

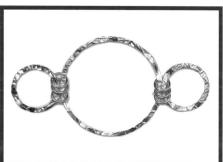

2 Repeat step 1 to attach another gold hoop to the silver hoop.

3 On each end, use a gold jump ring and two silver jump rings to attach a silver hoop.

4 On each end, use a gold jump ring and two silver jump rings to attach gold hoops until the necklace is within 2 in. (5cm) of the finished length. End with a gold hoop.

5 On one end, attach a silver jump ring, a gold jump ring, and a lobster claw clasp. On the other end, use a gold jump ring and two silver jump rings to attach a gold hoop as in step 4.

1 **bead-and-hoop earrings** • On a head pin, string a 4mm bicone crystal, a metal bead, and a 4mm bicone. Make a wrapped loop (Basics).

2 On a head pin, string a 6mm bicone crystal. Make a wrapped loop. Repeat.

3 Open a jump ring (Basics). Attach the bead units and a hoop. Close the jump ring.

4 Use two jump rings to attach the dangle and the loop of an earring wire. Make a second earring to match the first.

1 **two-hoop earrings** • Open a gold jump ring (Basics). Attach two hoops. Close the jump ring.

2 Attach a silver jump ring on each side of the gold jump ring.

3 Attach a silver jump ring to one hoop. Use a gold jump ring to attach the silver jump ring and the loop of an earring wire. Make a second earring to match the first.

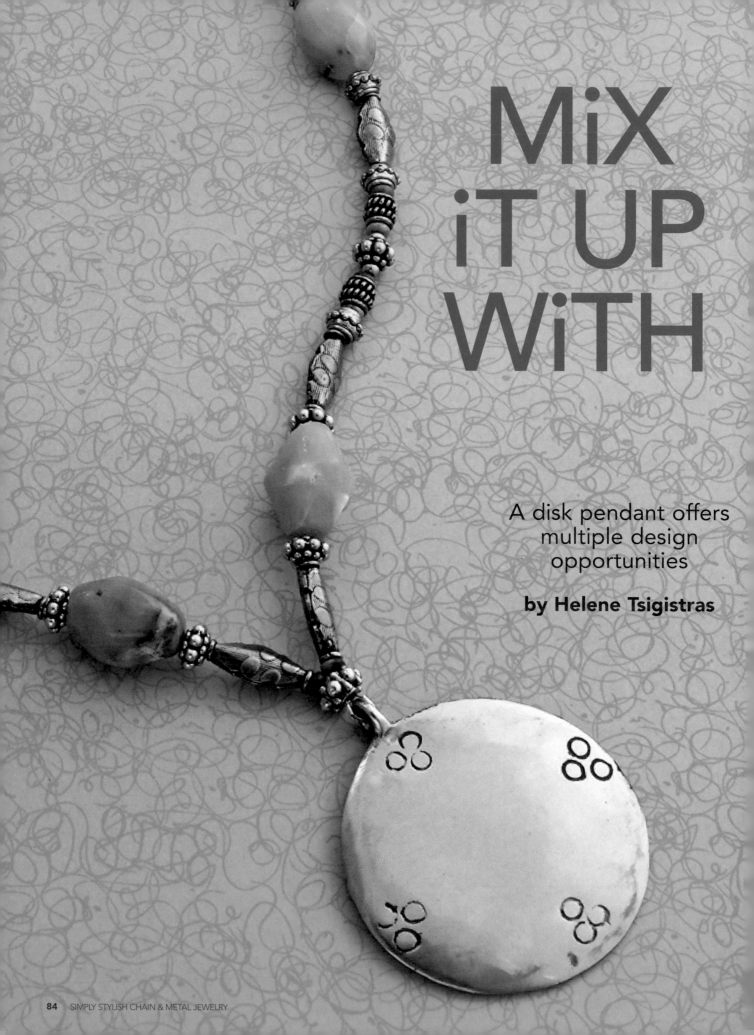

MiX iT UP WiTH

A disk pendant offers multiple design opportunities

by Helene Tsigistras

This brass pendant is a *melong*. Tibetan ritual items like this mirror are used by lamas, astrologers, and shamans. Design around a grand focal piece by incorporating copper and brass rondelles, or string a single type of metal. Whether you dress up the disk with kindred metals or mix things up a bit, your necklace will shine.

METAL

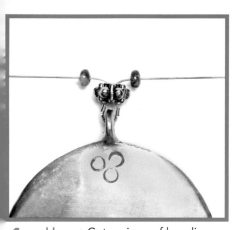

1 necklace • Cut a piece of beading wire (Basics, p. 5). Center a Wire Guardian and a pendant on the wire. Over both ends, string a metal rondelle. On each end, string a 4mm rondelle.

2 On each end, string a metal tube bead, a metal rondelle, a nugget, and a metal rondelle.

3 a On each end, string a metal tube bead. Alternate five metal rondelles with four 4mm rondelles.
  b Repeat steps 2 and 3a. String a tube and a metal rondelle. Alternate metal rondelles with 4mm rondelles until the strand is within 1 in. (2.5cm) of the finished length.

4 On each end, string: 4mm rondelle, crimp bead, 3mm spacer, Wire Guardian, half of a clasp. Check the fit, and add or remove beads from each end if necessary. Go back through the beads just strung and tighten the wire. Crimp the crimp bead (Basics) and trim the excess wire.

Supply List

necklace 22 in. (56cm)
- 50–60mm disk pendant (Tibetan Spirit, tibetanspirit.com)
- 10 18–22mm metal tube beads
- 4 15–20mm gemstone nuggets
- 31–35 10mm metal rondelles, 23–25 in brass, 8–10 in copper
- 18–20 4mm gemstone rondelles
- 2 3mm spacers
- flexible beading wire, .014 or .015
- 2 crimp beads
- 3 Wire Guardians
- toggle clasp
- chainnose or crimping pliers
- diagonal wire cutters

earrings
- 4 10mm metal rondelles
- 6 4mm gemstone rondelles
- 2 1½-in. (3.8cm) decorative head pins
- pair of earring wires
- chainnose pliers
- roundnose pliers
- diagonal wire cutters

1 earrings • On a head pin, string: 4mm rondelle, metal rondelle, 4mm, metal, 4mm. Make a plain loop (Basics).

2 Open the loop of an earring wire (Basics) and attach the dangle. Close the loop. Make a second earring to match the first.

DESIGN ALTERNATIVE
To keep the focus on this pendant's intricate details, the background beads stay neutral.

TIP
Experiment with shapes. It's not necessary for the rondelles to match.

DESIGN ALTERNATIVE
These very different metal pendants are Helene's favorites. "I love exotic looks," she says.

Contributors

Linda Augsburg is Senior Editor/Online for *BeadStyle*, *Bead&Button*, and *Art Jewelry* magazines. Contact her through Kalmbach Books.

A world traveler, **Rupa Balachandar** likes to create jewelry that makes a statement. She regularly travels through Asia looking for components to make her jewelry and is pleased to share her finds through her Web site, rupab.com. Contact her via e-mail at info@rupab.com.

Julie Boonshaft describes herself as an aspiring jewelry designer and a mom to four amazing kids. Her fondness for architecture — a mathmetically precise form of design — drew her to the art of making jewelry. Contact Julie via e-mail at julie@julieboonshaftjewelry.com, or visit julieboonshaftjewelry.com.

Nina Cooper says she feels very lucky to have inspiring materials close at hand. She likes to work in her new office — the first private workspace she's had in 25 years. Contact her at Nina Designs, 800-336-6462, via e-mail at nina@ninadesigns.com, or visit ninadesigns.com.

Erin Dolan learned to make jewelry when she worked as Editorial Assistant for *BeadStyle* magazine. Contact her via e-mail at erin.e.c.dolan@gmail.com.

Lorelei Eurto works full time in an art museum in upstate New York and has been creating jewelry part time since 2006. Visit her online at lorelei1141.etsy.com or artfire.com/users/lorelei1141. You can also visit her blog, where she shares an inside look at what she's working on, at lorelei1141.blogspot.com.

Naomi Fujimoto is Senior Editor of *BeadStyle* magazine and the author of *Cool Jewels: Beading Projects for Teens*. Visit her blog at cooljewelsnaomi.blogspot.com, or contact her via e-mail at nfujimoto@beadstyle.com.

Contact **Rebekah Gough** via e-mail at enna@fusionbead.com.

Lauren M. Hadley's biggest beading challenge is finding superior materials, especially high-quality semiprecious gemstones cut into unique shapes. Her inspiration always comes from the contour, color, and texture of the materials she uses. Contact her at mariemarie103@aol.com or visit mariemarie.etsy.com.

Contact **Heidi Hermreck** in care of Pam Israel at Via Murano, via e-mail at pam@viamurano.com.

Cathy Jakicic is Editor of *BeadStyle* magazine and the author of the book *Hip Handmade Memory Jewelry*. She has been creating jewelry for more than 15 years. Contact her via e-mail at cjakicic@beadstyle.com.

Armed with his mantra, "What are you gonna make today?," **Steven James** incorporates beads and jewelry making into home décor and everyday living. Visit his Web site, macaroniandglitter.com, or follow him at facebook.com/stevenjames.

Jane Konkel is Associate Editor of *BeadStyle*, and contributed several new designs to the book *Bead Journey*. Contact her via e-mail at jkonkel@beadstyle.com.

Carol McKinney is a jewelry designer from Amarilla, Texas. After designing mostly necklaces and bracelets, Carol plans to branch out into earrings soon. Contact her at lemon.leopard@hotmail.com or visit lemonleopard.com.

Formerly Editorial Associate of *BeadStyle*, **Lindsay Mikulsky** is currently pursuing a career in education. Contact her at lindsayrose5@gmail.com.

Brenda Schweder is the author of *Vintage Redux* and *Junk to Jewelry*. Her next book, *Iron Wire Jewelry*, is scheduled for release in fall 2010. A frequent *BeadStyle* contributor, Brenda has also been published in *Bead&Button* and *Art Jewelry* magazines. She currently serves as a CRYSTALLIZED™ Swarovski Elements Ambassador. Contact her via e-mail at b@brendaschweder.com, or visit her Web site, brendaschweder.com.

Helene Tsigistras's jewelry has been featured in *BeadStyle* and *Bead&Button* magazines. She has also contributed designs to several books, including *Easy Birthstone Jewelry*. Contact her via e-mail at htsigistras@kalmbach.com.

A hobbyist turned businesswoman, **Gretta Van Someren's** passion for jewelry design continues to grow and evolve. Her designs have been seen on television, featured in numerous magazines, and worn by celebrities. Contact her via e-mail at gretta@atterg.com or visit her Web site, atterg.com.